GW01524099

new livingroom design

daab

Andy Marcus | Denise Turner House	8
Arthur de Matttos Casas | Arpoador Penthouse	12
Bembé + Dellinger | Kaufmann House	16
Bleher Architects | Presche House	20
Budji Living | House in Bangkok	26
Buratti + Battiston Architects | Caccialepori Apartment	30
Carlos Mir | White Serenity	34
Caroline Schneider-Rodeck | House for a Family	40
Charles Deaton, Architect; Nicholas Antonopoulos, Architect Restauration; Charlee Deaton, Interior Design | Sculpture House	46
Cho Slade Architecture | Houchhouser Apartment	50
Conran & Partners | Forest Apartment	54
Enric Ruiz and Olga Subirós / Cloud 9 | Studio / Residence	58
Estrella Salieti | Curves	64
Florence Lim | Florence Lim House	70
GCA Arquitectes Associats | Vives-Escarmis Loft	76
Giovanni Schiavone | Villa Schiavone	82
Héctor Ruiz Velázquez and Javier García | House in Madrid	86
Holzer Kobler Architekturen | Room in a Room	90
Legorreta Arquitectos | Casa Lucía	94
Legorreta Arquitectos | Casa Víctor	98
LKD Concepts | Lilia Konrad Livingroom	104
Lucy Humbly, Interior Designer | The Bridge Penthouse	108
Miquel Adrià, Isaac Broid & Michel Rojkind | F2 House	112
Olga Vidal Interiorismo | Flat in Barcelona	116
Oriol Moyá Gimó | House in Doctor Rizal Street	120
Pankaj Patel | Tara Bernerd Flat	126
Philippe Starck´s Studio | Flat in Buenos Aires	132
RCR Aranda Pigem Vilalta Arquitectes Margarida House	138
Robin Rout | Robin Rout Ice	142
SJB Interiors | Beach House	148
SJB Interiors | Melbourne Penthouse	152
Salvio Parisi | Atelier / Studio Parisi	156
Sandra de Keller, designer | + White	160
Sanierung + Ausfstockung: **Architekten Carlos Zwick** | Zwick Loft	164
Tree Pte Ltd | Pigeon-Holed Apartment	170
VX Design | Ian Chee Flat	174
WORK AD | Gray Loft	182

El salón es tradicionalmente el lugar de la casa donde se han organizado las reuniones sociales y se han recibido las visitas, pero a lo largo de las últimas décadas ha experimentado abundantes cambios estéticos y de uso. Un ejemplo es la incorporación del cine en casa y otros equipos de tecnología punta dedicados al ocio, que han revolucionado la disposición y las formas del mobiliario que anteriormente se solía destinar a este ambiente. Por otro lado, el salón actual es también el lugar destinado al descanso, a la relajación y al disfrute de las aficiones personales. Por ello, una de las tendencias con más aceptación es aquella que subdivide el salón en dos áreas: una dedicada a los entretenimientos más tradicionales, como la charla y la lectura, y otra destinada a gozar de los objetos de tecnología más avanzada.

Le salon, en tant que lieu de la maison traditionnellement consacré aux réunions sociales et dans lequel "on recevait" les visites, a expérimenté de nombreux changements esthétiques et d'utilisation au cours des dernières décennies. Par exemple, l'incorporation du "ciné à la maison" et d'autres outils de technologie de pointe axés sur le loisir, a révolutionné la disposition et les formes du mobilier qui auparavant étaient généralement destinées à ces espaces familiaux. D'un autre côté, le salon actuel est aussi le lieu destiné au repos, à la relaxation et à la jouissance des hobbies personnels. C'est pour cela qu'une des tendances les plus en vue est celle qui sous-divise le salon en deux parties: l'une consacrée aux passe-temps les plus traditionnels comme la discussion et la lecture, et l'autre à l'usage des objets de technologie de pointe.

Il salotto é tradizionalmente la zona della casa dove si sono organizzate le riunioni sociali e il ricevimento delle visite, peró negli ultimi dcenni ha sperimentato forti cambiamenti estetici e d'uso. Un esempio é l'incorporazione del cinema in casa ed altri sistemi tecnologici innovativi dedicati all'ozio, che hanno rivoluzionato la disposizione e le forme dei mobili che in precedenza si solevano destinare a quest'ambiente. D'altra parte, il salotto attuale é anche il luogo destinato al riposo, al relax e agli hobby. Per questo una delle tendenze piú accettate é quella di suddividere il salotto in due aree: una dedicata alle attivitá tradizionali, come la conversazione e la lettura, e l'altra dedicata a sfruttare gli oggetti della tecnologia piú avanzata.

Das Wohnzimmer ist seit jeher der Ort des Beisammenseins und der Raum, in dem Gäste empfangen werden. In den letzten Jahrzehnten hat sich die „gute Stube" allerdings erheblich verändert: Das Heimkino und andere Errungenschaften der Unterhaltungselektronik haben eine Umgestaltung der Einrichtung bewirkt und sogar neue Möbeltypen hervorgebracht. Doch heute ist das Wohnzimmer auch ein Ort zum Ausruhen, Entspannen und um zu tun, was einem Freude macht. Eine der sich abzeichnenden Tendenzen ist daher die Unterteilung des Wohnzimmers in zwei Bereiche: Einer bleibt der Geselligkeit im traditionellen Sinne vorbehalten, d.h. der Unterhaltung, aber auch der Lektüre, während der andere Bereich sich ganz dem Genuss der technischen Möglichkeiten moderner Unterhaltungselektronik öffnet.

Traditionally, the living room has been the domestic setting for social gatherings and the reception of guests. Over the last decades however, it has experienced many changes with respect to aesthetics and use. One example is the incorporation of movies at home and other technological systems devoted to leisure that have revolutionized the layout and forms acquired by furnishings that have always formed part of this room. In addition, the contemporary living room is also a place in which to rest, relax and enjoy personal hobbies. For this reason, one of the most common and popular trends consists of dividing the living room into two areas: one designated to the more conventional entertainment of conversation and reading, and the other devoted to offering the pleasures made possible by state-of-the-art technology.

Andy Marcus | West Hollywood, USA
Denise Turner House
Palm Desert, USA | 2002

Arthur de Mattos Casas | São Paulo, Brazil
Arpoador Penthouse
São Paulo, Brazil | 2002

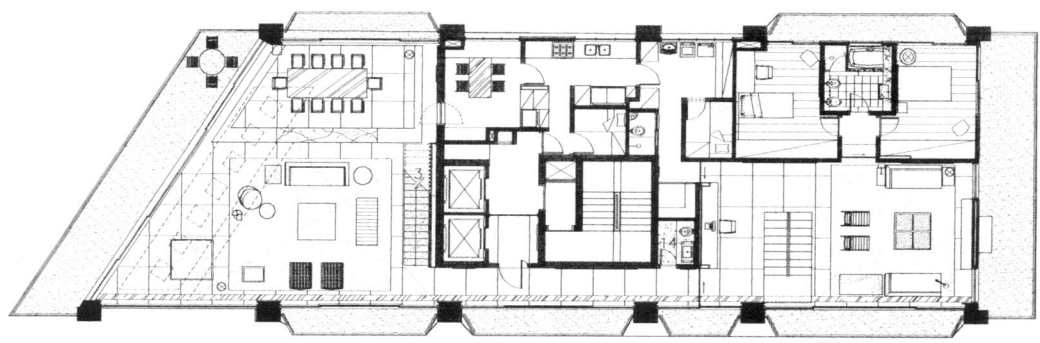

Bembé + Dellinger | Greifenberg, Germany
Kaufmann House
Greifenberg, Germany | 2003

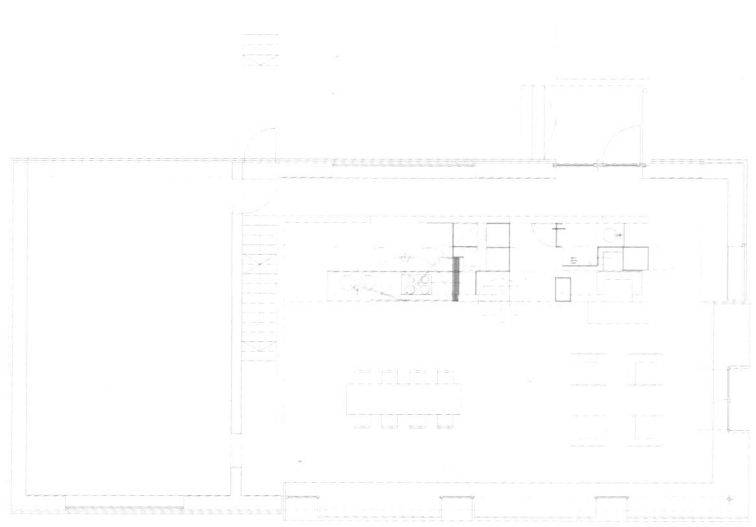

Bleher Architects | Remseck, Germany
Presche House
Stuttgart, Germany | 2001

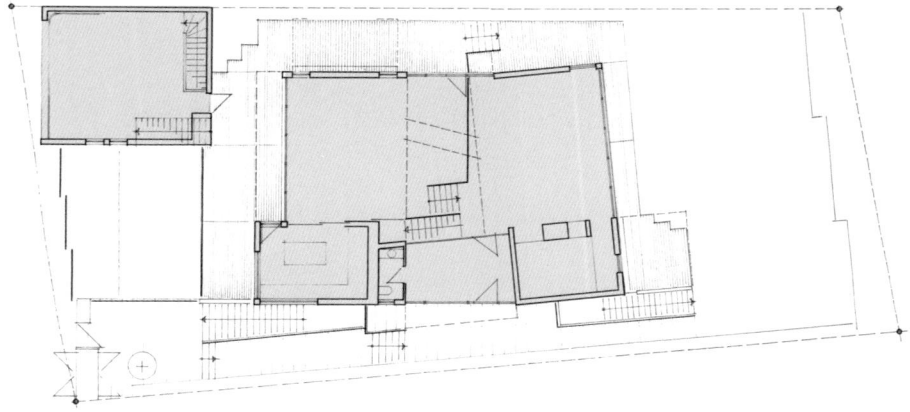

Budji Living | Bangkok, Thailand
House in Bangkok
Bangkok, Thailand | 2003

Buratti + Battiston Architects | Milan, Italy
Caccialepori Apartment
Milan, Italy | 2002

Carlos Mir | Barcelona, Spain
White Serenity
Barcelona, Spain | 2003

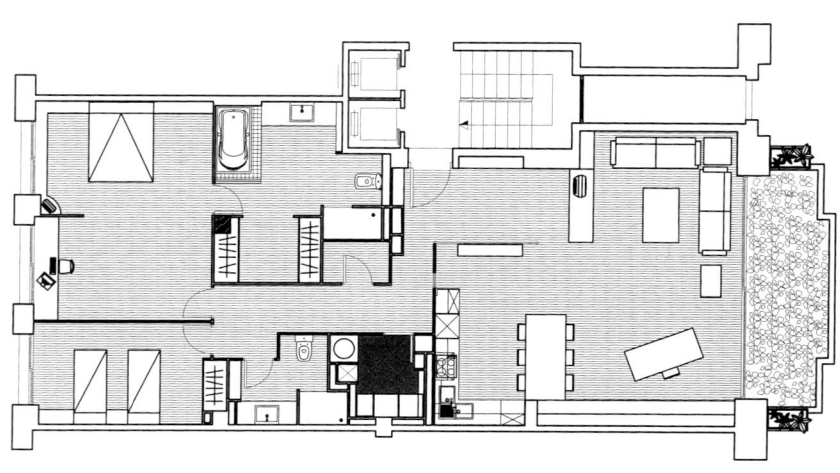

Caroline Schneider-Rodeck | Cologne, Germany
House for a Family
Cologne, Germany | 2002

**Charles Deaton, Architect; Nicholas Antonopoulos,
Architect Restauration; Charlee Deaton, Interior Design | Colorado, USA**
Sculpture House
Denver, USA | 2000

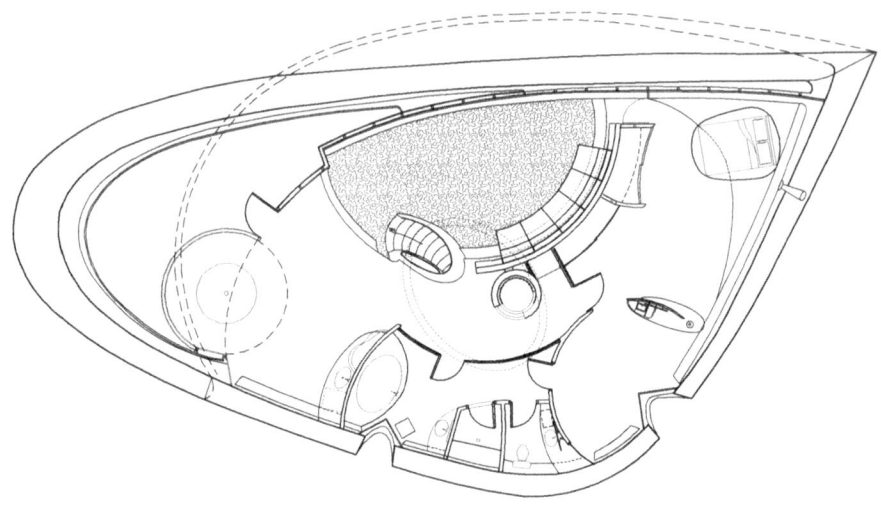

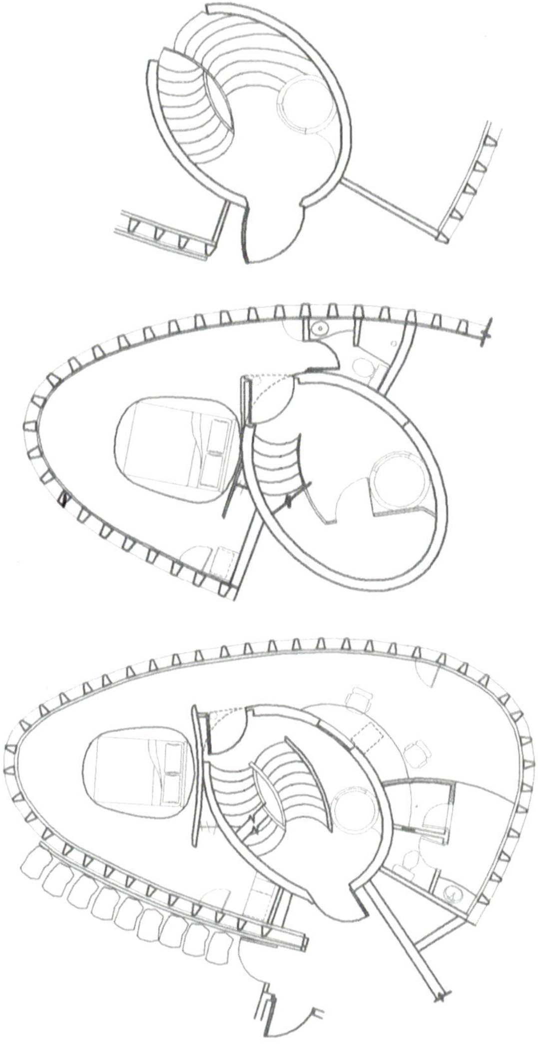

49

Cho Slade Architecture | New York, USA
Houchhouser Apartment
New York, USA | 2003

Conran & Partners | London, UK
Forest Apartment
Tokyo, Japan | 2003

Enric Ruiz and Olga Subirós / Cloud 9 | Barcelona, Spain
Studio / Residence
Barcelona, Spain | 2003

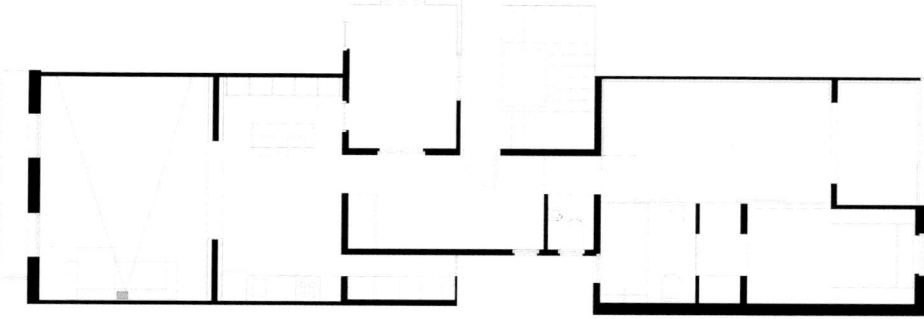

Estrella Salieti | Barcelona, Spain
Curves
Barcelona, Spain | 2003

Florence Lim | London, UK
Florence Lim House
London, UK | 2003

GCA Arquitectes Associats | Barcelona, Spain
Vives-Escarmis Loft
Barcelona, Spain | 2003

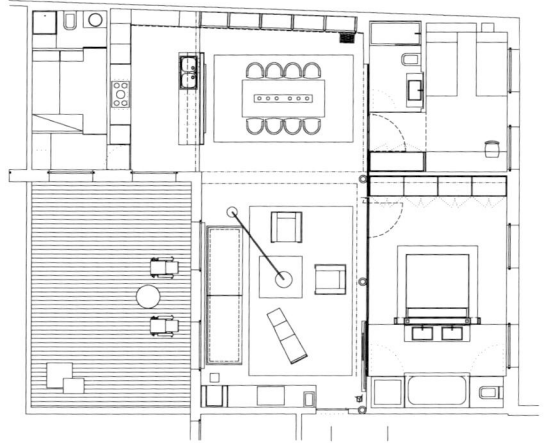

Giovanni Schiavone | Caserta, Italy
Villa Schiavone
Caserta, Italy | 2003

Héctor Ruiz Velázquez and Javier García | Madrid, Spain
House in Madrid
Madrid, Spain | 2003

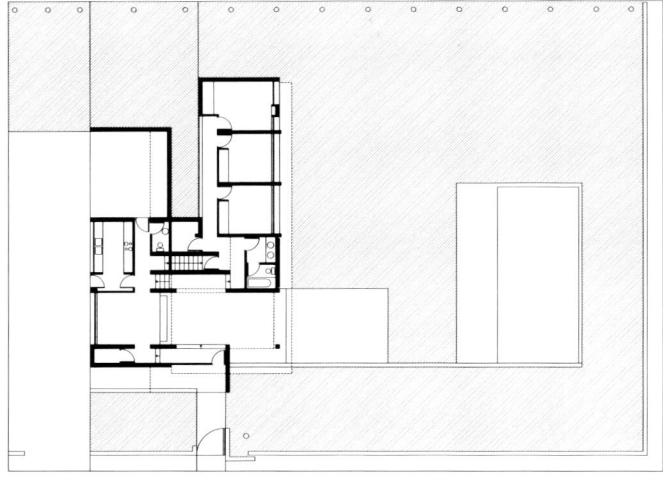

Holzer Kobler Architekturen | Zurich, Switzerland
Room in a Room
Berlin, Germany | 2001

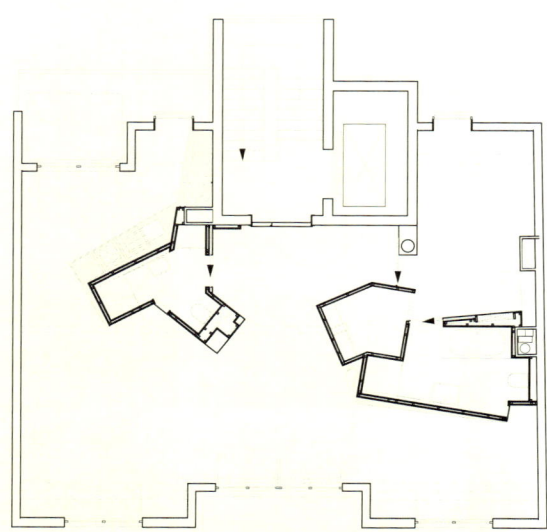

Legorreta Arquitectos | México DF, México
Casa Lucía
México DF, México | 2003

Legorreta Arquitectos | México DF, México
Casa Víctor
Valle de Bravo, México | 2003

LKD Concepts | Zurich, Switzerland
Lilia Konrad Livingroom
Zurich, Switzerland | 2001

Lucy Humbly, Interior Designer | London, UK
The Bridge Penthouse
London, UK | 2003

Miquel Adrià, Isaac Broid & Michel Rojkind | Colonia Nápoles, México
F2 House
Sayavena, México | 2001

Olga Vidal Interiorismo | Barcelona, Spain
Flat in Barcelona
Barcelona, Spain | 2002

Oriol Moyá Gimó | Barcelona, Spain
House in Doctor Rizal Street
Barcelona, Spain | 2001

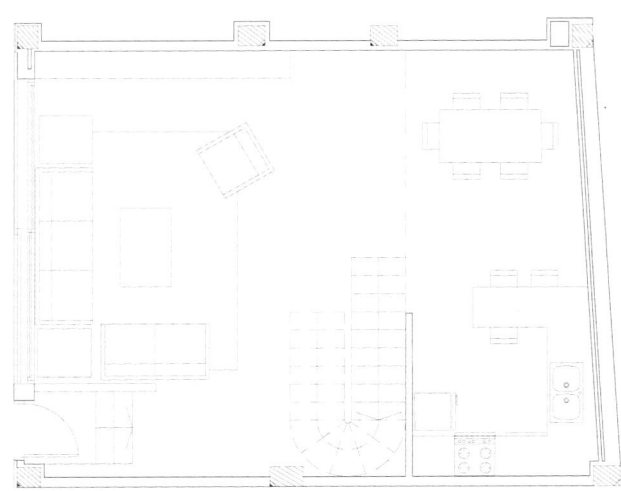

Pankaj Patel | London, UK
Tara Bernerd Flat
London, UK | 2002

Philippe Starck´s Studio | Paris, France
Flat in Buenos Aires
Buenos Aires, Argentina | 2003

RCR Aranda Pigem Vilalta Arquitectes | Girona, Spain
Margarida House
Girona, Spain | 2003

Robin Rout | London, UK
Robin Rout Ice
London, UK | 2001

SJB Interiors | Melbourne, Australia
Beach House
Mornington, Australia | 2002

SJB Interiors | Melbourne, Australia
Melbourne Penthouse
Melbourne, Australia | 2004

Salvio Parisi | Pozzuoli, Italy
Atelier / Studio Parisi
Pozzuoli, Italy | 2003

Sandra de Keller, designer | Barcelona, Spain
+ White
Barcelona, Spain | 2003

Sanierung + Ausfstockung: Architekten Carlos Zwick | Berlin, Germany
Zwick Loft
Berlin, Germany | 2002

Tree Pte Ltd | Singapore, Singapore
Pigeon-Holed Apartment
Singapore, Singapore | 2003

VX Design | London, UK
Ian Chee Flat
London, UK | 2003

WORK AD | New York, USA
Gray Loft
New York, USA | 2002

Andy Marcus. A.L.M. Interior Design
1041 North Sweetzer Avenue, West Hollywood
CA 90069, USA
P +1 213 716 9797
F +1 323 650 8204
alminteriordesign@earthlink.net
Denise Turner House
Photos: © Werner Huthmacher

Arthur de Mattos Casas
Rua Capivari 160, Pacaembú, São Paulo, SP, Brazil
P +55 11 3664 7700
Arpoador Penthouse
Photos: © Studio Arthur de Mattos Casas

Bembé + Dellinger
Am Schloß, 86926 Greifenberg, Germany
P +39 08 192 99 99 12
mail@bembe-dellinger.de
Kaufmann House
Photos: © Artur / Stefan Mueller-Naumann

Bleher Architects
Goldbergweg 34, 71686, Remseck, Germany
P +49 7146 9541
F +49 7146 9594
lub@uoregon.edu
Presche House
Photos: © Artur / Roland Halbe

Budji Living
7 soi Sang-Ngern (Thonglor 25)' Sukhumvit 55 Rd.,
Klongton-Nua, Wattana, Bangkok, Thailand
P (662) 712 9833
F (662) 712 9834
House in Bangkok
www.budjibangkok.com
Photos: © Zapaimages / Agi Simoes

Buratti + Battiston Architects
Via Grigna 22, 20020 Busto Garolfo, Milan, Italy
P +39 0331 569575
F +39 0331 569063
www.burattibattiston.it
Caccialepori Apartment
Photos: © Matteo Piazza

Carlos Mir
C/ Marqués de Monistrol 17, 08960 Sant Just Desvern
Barcelona, Spain
P +34 93 4733 124
F +34 93 4700 629
carlosmir@retemail.es
White Serenity
Photos: © Montse Garriga

Caroline Schneider-Rodeck
Alte Rheinstrasse 11, 50999 Cologne, Germany
P +49 2236 66707
F +49 2236 967227
Csr676@aol.com
House for a Family
Photos: © Artur / Birgit Amend

Charles Deaton, Architect; Nicholas Antonopoulos, Architect Restauration; Charlee Deaton, Interior Design
1033 South Gaylord Street, Denver, Co 80209, USA
praxarc@yahoo.com
Sculpture House
Photos: © Undine Pröhl

Cho Slade Architecture
367 East 10th St, New York, NY 1009, USA
P +01 212 677 6380
F +01 212 677 6330
www.sladearch.com
Houchhouser Apartment
Photos: © Jordi Miralles

Conran & Partners
22 Shad Thames, London SE1 2YU, UK
P +44 (0) 20 7403 88 99
F +44 (0) 20 7407 55 02
www.conranandpartners.com
Forest Apartment
Photos: © Conran & Partners

Enric Ruiz and Olga Subirós / Cloud 9
Passatge Mercader 10, 08008 Barcelona, Spain
P +34 93 215 05 53
www.e-cloud9.com
Studio / Residence
Photos: © Luis Ros

Estrella Salieti
Barcelona, Spain
Curves
Photos: © Montse Garriga

Florence Lim
London, UK
Florence Lim House
Photos: © Red Cover / Henry Wilson

GCA Arquitectes Associats
C/ Valencia 289, Bajos, 08009 Barcelona, Spain
P +34 93 476 18 00
F +34 93 476 18 06
www.gcaarq.com
Vives-Escarmis Loft
Photos: © Jordi Miralles

Giovanni Schiavone
Caserta, Italy
Villa Schiavone
Photos: © Roberto Pierucci / Sonia Cocozza

Héctor Ruiz Velázquez and Javier García
C/ Goya 42, 3º Izquierda, 28001 Madrid, Spain
P +34 91 577 45 18
grupomat@nauta.es
House in Madrid
Photos: © Pedro Mahamud

Holzer Kobler Architekturen
Ankerstrasse 3. CH-8004, Zurich, Switzerland
P + 41 1 240 52 00
F + 41 1 240 52 02
www.holzerkobler.ch
Room in a Room
Photos: © Simone Rosenberg

Legorreta Arquitectos
Palacio de Versalles 285 A, 11020 México
P +52 55 251 96 98
F +52 55 596 61 62
legorret@lmasl.com.mx
Casa Lucía
Casa Víctor
Photos: © Adam Buttler

LKD Concepts
Kämbelgasse 4, 08001 Zurich, Switzerland
P + 043 344 84 35
Lilia Konrad Livingroom
Photos: © Zapaimages / Reto Guntli

Lucy Humbly, Interior Designer
Aria House, 23 Craven Street (London Town),
London WC2N 5NT, UK
P +44 (0) 20 7839 55 88
www.londontownplc.co.uk
info@londontowngroup.co.uk
The Bridge Penthouse
Photos: © Carlos Domínguez

Miquel Adrià, Isaac Broid & Michel Rojkind
Chicago Suite 27 P.B., Colonia Nápoles 03810, México
P + 525 687 08 15
F + 525 536 23 86
F2 House
Photos: © Undine Pröhl

Olga Vidal Interiorismo
Apartado 512, 08188 Vallromanes, Spain
P / F +34 93 572 98 45
olgavidal91@hotmail.com
Flat in Barcelona
Photos: © José Luis Hausmann

Oriol Moyá Gimó
C/ Albigesos 9, Bajos 2°, 08024 Barcelona, Spain
P / F +34 93 213 02 16
440produccions@wol.es
Flat in Doctor Rizal Street
Photos : © Jordi Miralles

Pankaj Patel
London, UK
Tara Bernerd Flat
Photos: © Red Cover / Andreas von Einsiedel

Philippe Starck´s Studio
18 / 20, rue du Faubourg du Temple,
75001 Paris, France
P +33 (0) 1 48 07 54 54
F +33 (0) 1 48 07 54 64
www.philippe-starck.com
info@philippe-starck.com
Flat in Buenos Aires
Photos: © Ricardo Labougle / Ana Cardinale

RCR Aranda Pigem Vilalta Arquitectes
Passeig de Blay 34, 2°, 17800 Olot, Spain
Margarida House
Photos: © Montse Garriga

Robin Rout
London, UK
Robin Rout Ice
Photos: © Red Cover / Ken Hayden

SJB Interiors
25 Coventry St, Southbank VIC, 3006 Australia
P +61 3 9686 2122
F +61 3 9686 2125
www.sjb.com.au
interiors@sjb.com.au
Beach House
Melbourne Penthouse
Photos: © Tony Miller

Salvio Parisi
Pozzuoli, Italy
Atelier / Studio Parisi
Photos: © Roberto Pierucci / Donatella Bernabó

Sandra de Keller, designer
C/ Aribau 252, 1° 1ª, 08006 Barcelona, Spain
P +34 606 04 24 45
cyclopictures@hotmail.com
+ White
Photos: © Conrad White

Sanierung + Ausfstockung: Architekten Carlos Zwick
Torellstr. 7, 10243 Berlin, Germany
F +49 30 2934 3333
Zwick Loft
Photos: © Werner Huthmacher

Tree Pte Ltd
232 Bain Street, Unit 23-15, 180232 Singapore, Singapore
F +65 63 36 45 68 / 65 83 91 49
www.treestudio.com
Pigeon-Holed Apartment
Photos: © Kelley Chen

VX Design
London, UK
www.vxdesign.com
Ian Chee Flat
Photos: © Red Cover / Henry Wilson

WORK AD
200 Lafayette Street 6th Floor, New York, NY 10013, USA
P +212 343 2234
F +212 343 8953
www.workad.com
mmichalski@workad.com
Gray Loft
Photos: © Paul Warchol

copyright © 2004 daab gmbh

published and distributed worldwide by
daab gmbh
stadtwaldgürtel 57
d - 50935 köln

p +49-221-94 10 740
f +49-221-94 10 741

mail@daab-online.de
www.daab-online.de

publisher ralf daab
rdaab@daab-online.de

art director feyyaz
mail@feyyaz.com

editorial project by loft publications
copyright © 2004 loft publications

editor Encarna Castillo
layout Diego González
english translation Ana Cristina G. Cañizares
french translation Jean Pierre Layre Cassou
italian translation Grazia Suffritti
german translation Martin Fischer
copy editing Raquel Vicente Durán

printed in spain
Anman Gràfiques del Vallès, Spain
www.anman.com

isbn 3-937718-13-3
d.l.: B-27634-04

all rights reserved.
no part of this publication may be reproduced in any manner.